This catalog
belongs to
Vincent D. Smith

The Artist Project

Portraits of the Real Art World / New York Artists 1981 - 1990

PETER BELLAMY

Introduction by Neil Printz

For Vincent D. Smith.
Peter Bellamy
NYC
12/9/91

IN
PUBLISHING
NEW YORK, NEW YORK

IN PUBLISHING
NEW YORK, NEW YORK 1991

First Edition
Printed and bound in The United States of America

Library of Congress Cataloging-in-Publication Data

Bellamy, Peter
    The artist project : portraits of the real art world : New York artists. 1981—1990 / Peter Bellamy ; introduction by Neil Printz. 1st ed.
        p. cm.
    Includes index.
    ISBN 0-9625994-1-7 (hardcover) :   65 00
    1. Artists — New York (N.Y.) —Portraits. I. Title.
TR681.A7B45   1991
779'.2'092—dc20   91-35205
                                                   CIP

Design by Patti McQueen
10 9 8 7 6 5 4 3 2 1

CONTENTS

For my mother

INTRODUCTION

The Project

The individual does not make the history of his time, he both impresses himself on it and expresses its meaning. It is possible to record the historical physiognomic image of a whole generation and, with enough knowledge of physiognomy, to make that image speak in photographs. The historical image will become even clearer if we juxtapose pictures typical of the many different groups that make up human society, which together would carry the *expression of the time* and *the sentiments of their group.* The time and the group sentiment will be especially evident in certain individuals whom we can designate by the term "type." The same observations can be made about sports clubs, musicians, businesses and similar organizations. Thus the photographer with his camera can grasp the physiognomic image of his time. [Author's emphases]

August Sander, "The Nature and Development of Photography," Lecture [5], 1931

In 1910 when August Sander, a portrait photographer by training and trade, embarked on his mission to capture the "physiognomic images of his time," his project rested upon a particular premise regarding the nature of photographic truth. For Sander, as for most of the last century and for much of this, the photograph is understood as the registration of something that is, to become the record of something that has been.

More than painting or sculpture, but something like drawing, photography appears to be the first visual medium to have become directly implicated with time, its privileged relationship to the present engendering a reflex committed to documenting the past. For Sander, the practice of photography was situated unequivocally within the enterprise of history.

What might be considered as a germinal premise about the medium still obtains as a theoretical model, although its operation has been viewed problematically by some recent image makers. Stressing the way in which a photograph interprets what it represents, that it may select, enhance, or distort — and invariably it does — they have polemicized the practice, exposing the way photographs falsify conditions and conjure relations that have not quite been, fabricating new desires for that which has never been before.

But if a photograph can invent what has never been, it cannot deny what has been, if it once has been before the lens. Presences registered within the photographic image have necessarily existed somewhere and at one time. "And when the photograph was taken, we were in it." (Gertrude Stein, from *In Circles,* by Al Carmines). When the photograph is taken, something has been taken, an actuality has been captured and transferred, the existence of which thereafter becomes incontrovertible.

This is the photograph's irreducible quotient of truth: what has been photographed has in some way existed. It may continue to exist for a period of time after the photograph has been taken — although it does not necessarily — but it did exist at one time, if only for what we might specify as "the moment." Yet, before it characterizes the way things have been, a photograph makes manifest the way they have *not* been. It affirms suppressed data. As such photography's practice may address a social usage arguably more urgent than expression. Assembled collectively, photographs function as an archive of gathered testimony, establishing that "this has been," or even that "this has been so."

August Sander's encyclopedic project, which he called *Man of the Twentieth Century*, was never completed. Almost twenty-five years into it, in 1934 the Nazis interrupted his work, confiscating and destroying a popular edition of the work which he had published in 1929 as *Face of Our Time*. Not only did his physiognomic image of his time not conform to the racial reductivism of the "pure Aryan type" after which the Third Reich was then fashioning its image, Sander's survey of faces assembled abundant and eloquent sociological evidence to the contrary, of Aryans that were other.

Had the Nazis not suppressed Sander's portrait photography, deterring him from thinking of ever completing it, one can only speculate upon how much longer he might have kept at it. How many more faces that reflected and expressed the conditions of their historical time and the particular characteristics of their group affiliation would he have felt it necessary to photograph? When would he have terminated his project, believing that he had assembled enough individuals from which to extrapolate the generality and structure of the whole, constituted as a collectively inclusive but historically bounded portrait of the society of his time?

The Artist Project, undertaken by Peter Bellamy over a ten-year period between 1981 and 1990, participates in the kind of historical operation articulated in photography that Sander formulated so decisively. To recapitulate our opening citation:

The historical image will become even clearer if we juxtapose pictures typical of the many different groups that make up human society, which together would carry the expression of the time and the sentiments of their group.

August Sander, *The Painter Gottfried Brockmann* (Cologne 1924)
Courtesy of *The Archives of August Sander—Gard Sander, Köln, Germany and The Museum of Modern Art, NYC*

By differentiating group affiliations according to profession, affinity, class and social position, Sander parsed the social body into aggregates of designated types who embodied the salient characteristics of what he called the "group sentiment." Juxtaposed, they assembled a kind of group portrait that expressed the time, crystallized into an image of the historical moment. Like the late Victorian he was, Sander worked from the positivist assumption that the meaning of the whole might be arrived at by induction, calibrated from a "correct" ratio of its parts. His project postulated a system of representational authority.

Although Peter Bellamy seems to share Sander's conviction about photographic practice grounded in historical vision, and one that would link the "expression of the time" to the "sentiments of the group," he does not share into Sander's statistical and structural rationales. Bellamy's subjects are all artists. Individually, each subject bears witness to the idiosyncrasy of a personal presence, while collectively sharing membership in a professional affiliation, that never pretends to constitute definitively or approximate the constructed unity of group sentiment. For Bellamy, one portion of society, one group, or even one individual may never stand in proxy for absent others. The artists he has photographed and those whose portraits he includes here are not offered to us as exemplars from whom we may construe the composition and character of contemporary art society, let alone contemporary society. Rather, Bellamy proposes that they *are* contemporary society. Bellamy may have concentrated his attention upon a single group, but from the first he has envisioned something less and more than the portrait of a *metier*. His driving insight has been that he is "photographing society."

The Artist Project began with the portraits of a handful of artists. Asking each artist to suggest five others that he might photograph, Bellamy then proceeded over a period of ten years to photograph over 600 artists living and working in New York City. This "artist's choice" methodology democratized the selection process, diffusing a single aesthetic or social propensity towards identifiable "types" among the participants themselves. Though seemingly simple enough, however, it contains the germ of its own numerical juggernaut. As Bellamy proceeded and matrixes of the number five fanned out in greater extension, the project's initial impulse was transformed from a straightforward, even casual trajectory into densities of accumulating complexity.

The selection of artists represented in this book, itself a selection of the artists represented in the project, maps a network of referrals rather than pretending to approximate a cross-section whose contours more or less correspond to those of the whole. This network was socially based: artists recommended others whom they knew, whose work they thought worthy of consideration, or more likely, they recommended artists who, for demographic, personal or picturesque reasons, they thought should be "represented" in *The Artist Project*. The project's sampling may be characterized not so much as random, as convivial and circumstantial; there are enough particularities here to interrupt any generalities about the nature of the group.

The project's subjects comprise a broad social range of age, gender, race and fame. Their physiognomies expose varying conditions of age and youth, color and "white-ness;" some are male, some female, some are well-known (but certainly none will ever again belong to that impossible category carelessly identified as "unknown"). If there are biases reflected within the project and among the photographs included here — and inevitably there are, as there must be in any method of selection — its point of view has tended to suppress such factors of popular recognition as artistic notability and notoriety.

The invention of photography coincided with the birth of modern art. This is now cliche, but what might interest us here is not the formative influences of one upon the other, but their historical mutuality. Parallel to the history of modern art is a complementary commentary in the form of a photographic inventory of modernism's great practitioners: an anthology of innovators and pioneers, modern art's hall of fame. From Nadar, Man Ray, Brassai, and André Kertesz, among others, the *chefs de l'ecole de Paris* have become lionized and even grown familiar to us.

In their capacity as inspired, artists have become the sacred monsters of modern life. They have proven to be irresistible subjects for photography, inflecting its documentary gaze with fascination. These famous and infamous men and women of genius have been served up to a notional public of culturally passive spectators, whose "looks" they are invited to see and thereafter recognize, to scrutinize and thereafter judge. In so doing, photography has collaborated with the myth of the reciprocity of cultural distinction and social aberration.

Only somewhat less rhetorically, photographs such as the famous series by Hans Namuth showing Jackson Pollock painting a picture have been instrumental in fashioning and propagating a particularly masculinized and heroic imagery for the "new" American art of the post-war era. Here, action displaces attention from the consumption of a portrait of essentialized greatness in order to transmit a theatricalized rendering of experience that may be crystallized into a body of imagery, or better yet into a single image.

Bellamy's project necessarily avoids and critiques the fictive dimensions of art's photographic context by addressing itself to issues of the social representation of artists. In Sander's work, each portrait evinced a kind of autonomy, because each photographed individual appeared to embody the whole of the project in a concentrated form. Bellamy's portraits rarely exhibit that kind of self-sufficiency; his photographs pivot on the power and the prosaic repetition of so many personal encounters. Here, the private space of each artist's studio becomes a variously animated social space in which Bellamy, as photographer and fellow artist, must be received, met with and engaged.

The Photographs

Might we look *through* these photographs? Is there a privileged point of entry into this assembly of portraits, a preferred path of access through them? In the spirit of the project, Bellamy has presented them here alphabetically, deflecting premeditated cultural strategies of hierarchy, classification, analogy or formal composition. He has also inserted captions for each image, predicated not only upon the subject but upon the dynamic of the encounter between subject and observer.

In the seventeenth century, Constantin Huygens, a rather learned and well-connected gentleman, criticized a portrait of one of his relations by Rembrandt. He observed that the portrait resembled the sitter, but insisted upon a curious disclaimer: those who knew the subject (as he did) would know that it wasn't his face they were seeing in the portrait, that the portrait wasn't him. The scholar David Freedberg has suggested that Huygens' comments need not be construed as a negative assessment of Rembrandt, from whom he became estranged, but that they might have served and might still serve as the basis for a theory of portraiture. Verisimilitude may capture a visual likeness, but it must fall short of life-likeness, as the portrait can neither move nor speak. A portrait of the subject speaking, the "speaking portrait," invests the likeness based on appearances with an appeal to another sense, hearing, and with a greater claim to a liveliness that ultimately empowers the representation. Beyond those physiognomic attributes of appearance, so prized by Sander in his typologies of professional caste, one point of departure *into* the 225 portraits comprising this selection from Bellamy's *The Artist Project* might involve us in this problem of liveliness. We would want to consider how each artist positions his or herself in relation to the gaze of Bellamy's camera and how he or she temporarily inhabits that extension of his or her personality represented by the space of the studio. Among so many portraits of people of such different appearance, we may begin with a system of mutually inclusive questions, full of imbrications. How many artists does Bellamy seize at just the "decisive moment" of liveliness that interrupts an argument or its exposition at mid-sentence and mid-gesture?

Look at the photograph of Richard Serra, for example. Examine how his looking becomes implicated with thinking and speaking, or having spoken. How many seem thus involved; how many remote, not looking, even dreamy, eyes closed, cigarette smoking? How many fold their arms across the chest in poses read as defensive or truculent? How many untended hands are clasped in laps? How many bodies contract tensely, or with intensity? How many smile?

How many are posed or have posed themselves with their work, barricaded behind it, posed seductively or tentatively in front of it? How many have staged charades or *tableaux vivants* with their work? How many are seen or let themselves be seen working? Are they actively working or resting, somewhere between engagement and repose? How many touch their work; how many examine it; how many look away? We may begin to examine what it is that we conventionally designate as work and how it is that artists have qualified the operations which they call work.

For an artist, famous, forgotten, or unrecognized, the photographic portrait constitutes an opportunity to consciously situate oneself — in analogy to one's work and to the nature of the work involved in one's work — before the public. In his book on photography, *Camera Lucida*, Roland Barthes, bemused and petulant, reflected upon the problems and the tropes of posing for the camera. Looking at André Kertesz' famous photograph of Mondrian, he wonders what Mondrian was thinking about, and how he was able to make himself look intelligent for the camera. In the improvised and invented environment of the studio, artist and photographer must contrive to look uncontrived, or in different circumstances, conspire to let the contrivances hang out.

The posed portrait, particularly of such practiced social performers as professional artists, bears a complex relationship to candor, one as much beset by codes of cultural role-playing as it may be illuminated by inadvertent revelations of character. Taylor Mead's portrait addresses this issue head-on. Tee-shirt emblazoned with a busty pinup, he apes its pose for the camera's record; smiling impishly at the disparities of glamour and squalor, his artist's life has excavated.

In the last analysis, we must ask ourselves what these photographs can tell us about artists. Our informal survey of opening questions begins to suggest how complex any order of classification would become, and how hopelessly inconclusive it would be to look for obtaining generalities. Yet surely we might find particular insights about certain artists, about the way they live and work. Such insights into art and artists' lives that they do grant us, however, are largely contingent upon the conditions of one's prior recognition of a subject's identity, the curiosity that such recognition arouses, and the interpretation that it accommodates and confirms. Although, here criteria of notoriety may yield to liveliness, it inescapably informs one's interpretation or lack of it. In this sense, I think we may learn very little, if by this we ask for something new.

In place of a system of inductive meaning or of particular-
ized readings of character, let me propose another in which
taxonomy and psycho-biography cede to the hermeneutical
operations of social intelligence. As individual presences,
Bellamy's subjects mostly subvert their punitive isolation;
aware of being watched, they invite participation in betray-
ing the fictions of "creative solitude," and in perpetuating
the fiction of liveliness. As a corporate body, we need not
reduce or generalize personal characteristics, except to say
that they are all artists, that they are here in number, that
their numbers are greater than the parameters of this book
and this project can apprehend. They are not all *here,* but
taken together, they would all be *there.*

During the catastrophic depression of the 1930s, under the
federally subsidized art projects of Franklin Roosevelt's New
Deal, not only were artists acknowledged as members of the
national work force, but for the first time in this country
their numbers were counted. The myth of their non-
productivity was rebutted, recuperating them from a mar-
ginal bohemianism to professional status in American
society. At times of cultural crisis — and the present may
surely be viewed as such a time — the fact that certain numbers are counted, that certain witnesses present themselves,
and that certain testimony is gathered, constitutes a polemic
of inclusion. In such a context and with compelling evidence,
Peter Bellamy's artist project advocates that we count, consider and contend with the presence of artists among us,
neither as mandarins nor as pariahs, but as rank and file
constituents of that much abused site, the body politic.
Neil Printz, 1991 ©

The Artist Project

I placed my entire being into this project for 10 years. I felt that nothing could stop me, but at the same time I was at my subjects' mercy. I was like a dog going after a treat: I went after the next picture as if my life depended on it. I scratched and whined at doors, howled for attention in my pursuit until I was granted access or was beaten away with sticks and stones, only to return again. I accept the moral responsibility for my pictures in terms of the effects the taking of them had on my victims. In capturing their likenesses I was after what they could not give: identity and environment. My response in the end could only be to be as purely truthful as possible, and perceive without prejudice. I hope I have done that. — Peter Bellamy

"A-1"

Anthony Clark, Jr.
A young graffiti artist who grew up on the subways.
For him, it was a creative process.
The Bronx, 1982

VITO ACCONCI

Very into Freud and la chose génitale.
In one of his performance pieces, he posed nude
with his genitals tucked between his legs, creating an imaginal woman.
The Brooklyn Waterfront, 1985

PETER AGOSTINI

He is like a Greek scholar and his young wife, Aphrodite.
Working in wet plaster of paris he has sculpted what is, to some, the inevitable theft:
the instinct's perception of its true self.
SoHo, 1987

DONALD ALBERTI

A minimalist.
Crosby Street, 1982

CANDIDA ALVAREZ

She makes her abstract art in a sunny studio overlooking the East River;
in the shadow of where this young Puerto Rican woman grew up.
The Brooklyn Waterfront, 1987

EMMA AMOS

Art is a personal journey, and artists often find other means
of support for themselves and their families.
Emma: a teacher, married, with children.
SoHo, 1987

To
Vincent
We're the REAL
ART World
Alright
Love,
Emma

MILET ANDREJEVIC

His erotic, pastoral scenes are made even more powerful
by a profound knowledge of the bone and muscle structure of the human figure.
Upper West Side, 1987

IDA APPLEBROOG

If one becomes one's creative image, then Ida is refreshing laughter
at the human condition in its seeming crisis.
SoHo, 1984

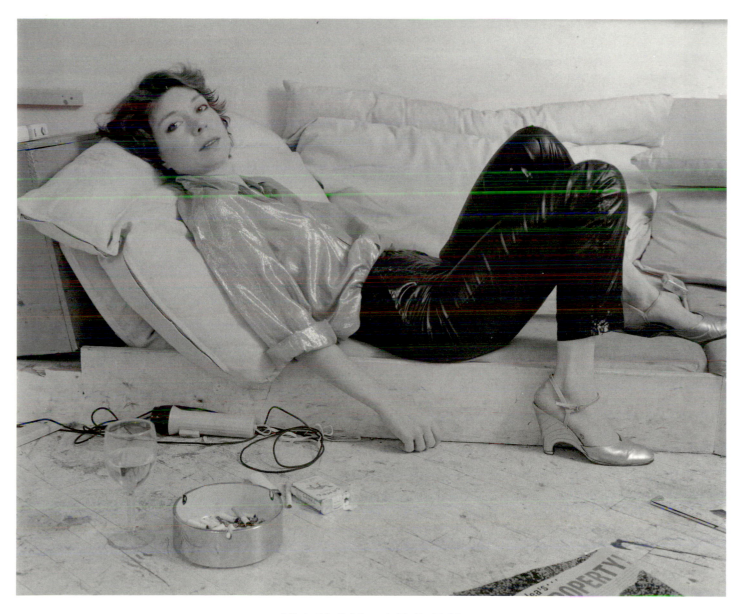

NANCY ARLEN

Arlen, working with glass, plastic, and fiberglass,
knows how to handle poison.
Tribeca, 1982

RICHARD ARTSCHWAGER

His view of life has a humorous clarity, as bright as that light behind him.
My camera took the magical image that Richard was not aware of.
The Lower East Side, 1984

ALICE AYCOCK

"I make enormous work and everyone expects me to be big and butch,
but as you can see, I am quite small and beautiful."
SoHo, 1985

DONALD BAECHLER

Creativity wraps this favorite son like a mantle.
He does very elegant drawings and wash paintings on large linen canvases.
The Financial District, 1982

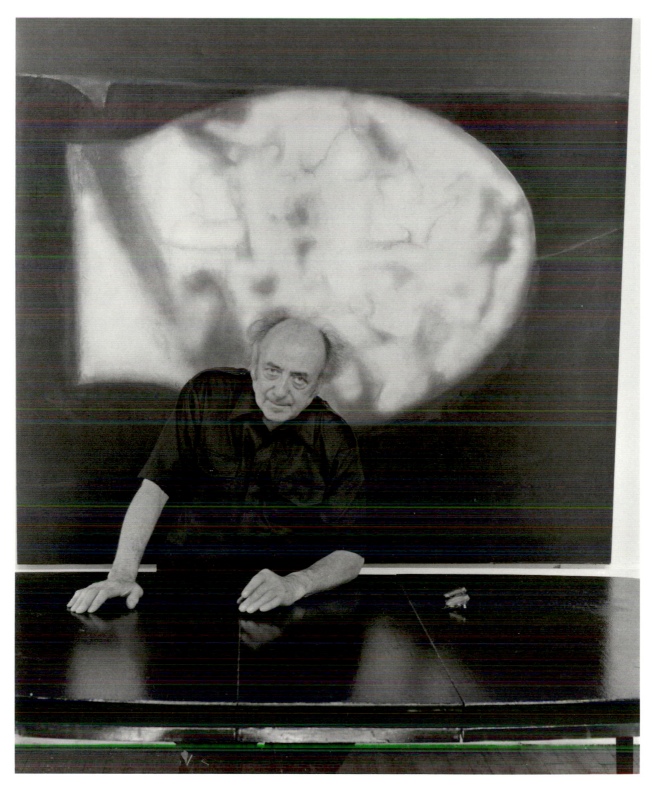

RUDOLF BARANIK

A European who fought on the beaches at D-Day,
he spoke to me of the bodies that were floating around him there.
Artists often open up to me.
What unforgettable times those are.
SoHo, 1984

WILL BARNET

His work is very graceful and elegant.
Gramercy Park, 1986

JACK BEAL

He has an archetypal basis for his notions of creativity:
a studio over the Hudson River,
a devoted following of young realists,
and a farm as sanity saver.
Tribeca, 1985

ROBERT BEAUCHAMP

He and his art are alike:
complex, charged with mystical qualities, charmed in the shamanistic sense.
West 30s, 1985

ANDREA BELAG

She is a moving abstractionist.
"The graphic and the calligraphic element in [my] work
has always been strong . . . What appeals to me in painting
about graphic information is that it is inherently two-dimensional,
and because of that, it seems a natural component of the visual language."
Tribeca, 1984

ADOLF BENCA

His paintings are either self portraits,
a la Rembrandt van Rijn with a shot of Sir Francis Bacon,
or epic struggles such as a huge series based on Moby Dick.
He strives for greatness.
West 58 Street, 1983

ROBERT BLACKBURN

His print shop is a port-of-call to many nationalities,
a place that makes you feel art as a universal language.
Chelsea, 1987

RONALD BLADEN

A member of the "Tenth Street Gang" with Franz Kline and Willem de Kooning.
He died of cancer in 1989, a few years after I took this photo.
One of his last and most important pieces is pictured here:
"Black Lightening."
West 20 Street, 1984

NELL BLAINE

Young and admired artist, then stricken with polio,
her work reflects the strength of her soul.
The Upper West Side, 1986

DIKE BLAIR

An easy going guy who makes abstract, yet precise, art.
SoHo, 1981

ANNIE BONNEY

She's not only an artist, astrologer, and spiritual advisor,
to many other artists she is also a good friend.
SoHo, 1985

RICHARD BOSMAN

His paintings are often sorrowful and savage.
Born in India, he said that when he closes his eyes, he is still there.
Tribeca, 1984

LOUISE BOURGEOIS

She is considered to be one of the great artists of this century.
She has an iron will, is a good friend, and loves jazz.
Brooklyn, 1986

NANCY BOWEN

She quotes Anais Nin — "The language of sex has yet to be invented,
for man's language is inadequate for the mysteries of woman's sensuality."
Tribeca, 1983

DAVID BOWES

He makes beautifully gentle images, like the gentleness in his face.
In him, the creative seems to be an achievement of love,
marked by imagination and beauty.
West 89 Street, 1985

HELENE BRANDT

Leonardo da Vinci flight sculpture on prepared ground.
Wards Island, 1983

FARRELL BRICKHOUSE

"Painting is like talking someone out of jumping off a bridge.
You can't promise a better world, you can only show you've stood out there too,
and found some reason not to leap."
Tribeca, 1985

JAMES ANDREW BROWN

Spiritual contentment in a high-tech world with
a unique choreographic sense of space.
New Jersey, 1987

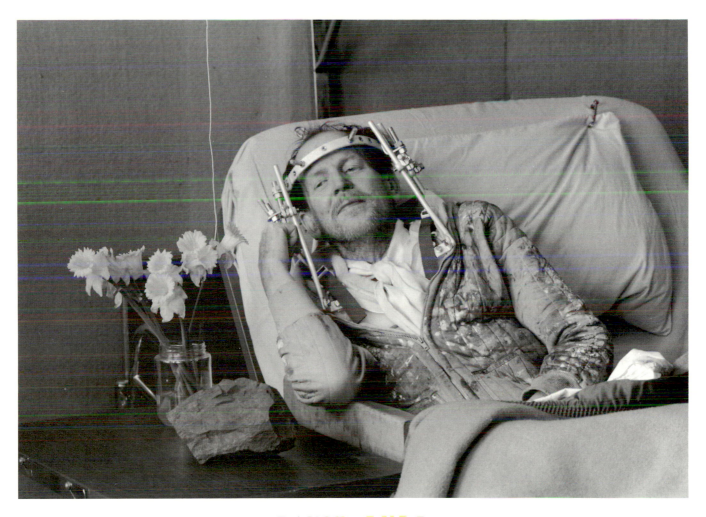

DAVID BUDD

The brace, from a broken neck, is like a crown of thorns
and his humor is a definite sign of strength.
This is one of my favorite photos
Park Avenue South, 1986

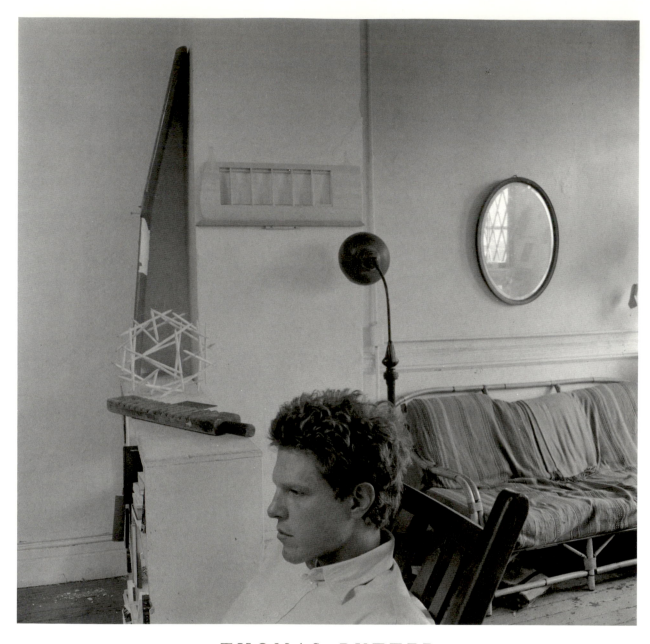

THOMAS BUTTER

His sculpture has helped legitimize fiberglass as a workable creative material,
taking what could only be expressed in drawing into the third dimension.
Chinatown, 1982

JOHN CAGE

If, as he says, the loud and rowdy noises of Manhattan are like music to him,
then his work in the visual arts must be portraits of silence.
The West Side, 1986

ANDREA CALLARD

To me she represents the feminine persona,
an absolutely vital part of the creative world.
Tribeca, 1983

GRETNA CAMPBELL

She teaches at Yale, a lovely woman, reflecting a fiery inner beauty.
This portrait is very honest.
West Broadway, 1986

ELLEN CAREY

The conflict between my photo and her self portrait is understandable;
in mine she has the flu.
SoHo, 1986

JAMES CASEBERE

He makes travel photos with a twist — he concocts the places himself and shoots them.
They are as seductive as new snow.
The Lower East Side, 1982

SARAH CHARLESWORTH

When I took this photo, she was living with Amos Poe and Joseph Kosuth.
Excitement came from those three strong energies being in the same space
and on top of the same ladder at the same time.
SoHo, 1982

LOUISA CHASE

*She gained fame very early for her art,
along with the pressure of the outer public
trying to invade and consume the inner private artist.
Tribeca, 1983*

HERMAN CHERRY

There is a comradery among older artists.
Having seen it all, they are familiar with the islands, are the chiefs of the tribes.
SoHo, 1986

TSENG KWONG CHI

He was a photographer who traveled the world, taking pictures of
himself dressed as an official of the Communist Party.
His death, in the late 80s, was related to AIDS.
As with all deaths, it deepened us.
Chelsea, 1982

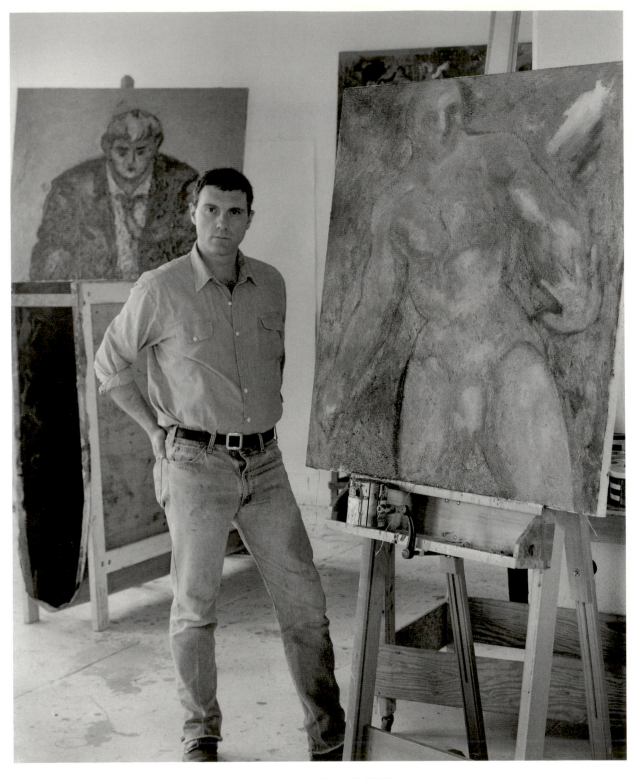

SANDRO CHIA

Full of conflict, very human, vital, successful —
he revives motifs from antiquity and adds a layer of humor.
Chelsea, 1984

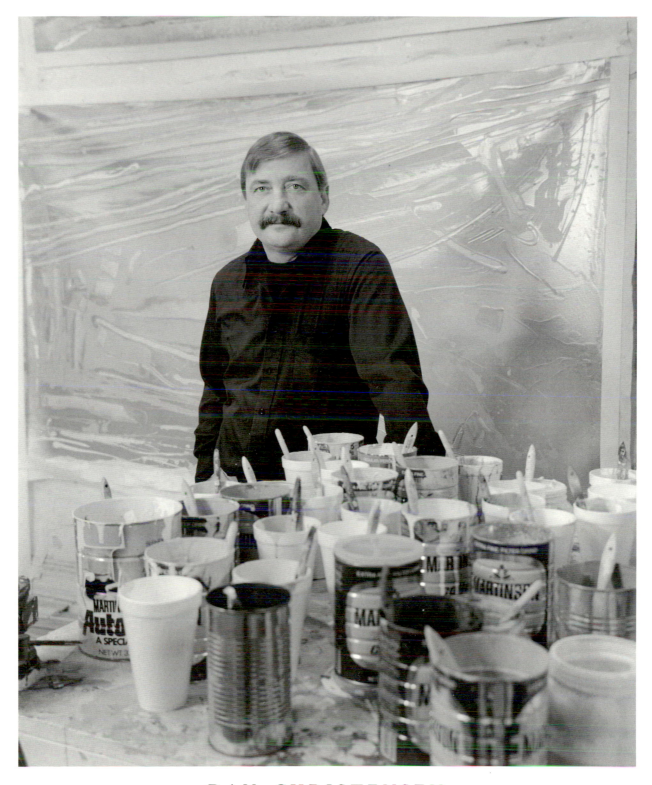

DAN CHRISTENSEN

"He is one of the painters on whom the course of American art depends."
— Clement Greenberg, *Art Critic*
Waverly Place, 1984

ED CLARK

He has a very strong sense of self.
Artistic minds always play with the things they love most.
Chelsea, 1987

ALPHAEUS COLE

At 108, Cole is the wisest, not to mention oldest, artist that I have ever photographed.
This shot was taken in the Chelsea Hotel where, forty years before, he made
a deal with the management — to give them three paintings in exchange for
not having his rent raised.
Perhaps that is why he was able to live so long.
Chelsea, 1986

GEORGE CONDO

An enfant terrible *of the art world.*
Parties hard, lives fast.
East Village, 1985

RONNIE CUTRONE

A child of Lou Reed,
Andy Warhol,
and Max's Kansas City Bar.
Westbeth, Greenwich Village, 1984

AVEL DE KNIGHT

A spirit of the night.
Greenwich Village, 1987

BRETT DE PALMA

*"The artist must take greater care than ever not to allow himself to be separated
from the real world and from humanity."*
— Henri Cartier-Bresson

*Judging by his studio on bustling Times Square,
in a rundown building filled with junkies,
Brett knows this.
Times Square, 1985*

PORFIRIO DIDONNA

A remarkably perceptive abstract painter and deeply reflective man.
He died during the 80s of a brain tumor.
Tribeca, 1982

SARI DIENES

Her instincts chose a path for her early in life;
one with passion.
SoHo, 1986

MARK DI SUVERO

He has made an enormous contribution of sculpture to the world;
the heart of industrial art — a heart of oil and steel.
Storm King Art Center, 1985

ORSHI DROZDIK

"She borrows from hard science in order to puncture its pretenses and self-importance . . .
Drozdik transforms art into something like an archaeology of consciousness, and peers
around the backside of the mind." — Edward Ball, *Art Critic*
Tribeca, 1986

VALENTINA DUBASKY

She believes in the pleasure principle, is very bold, loves animals.
The East Village, 1985

JOHN E. DUFF

An experimenter.
Always discovering what different materials can do;
his risk-taking has helped other artists become more innovative.
Chinatown, 1983

NANCY DWYER

A long time friend of Cindy Sherman.
They go out together dressed to kill — two New York dolls.
Greenwich Village, 1983

STEFAN EINS

This shot is a performance piece in itself.
The Bronx, 1985

STEPHEN ELLIS

He has gained a following as a writer, but his greatest passion is painting.
Nothing else comes close to it in his life.
The Financial District, 1985

BOB ELLISON

"The clatter of steel, stiffly-sprung speeding trucks, jackhammers, and the hiss of buses,
all crowding.
The anesthesia of oil-paint smell creeps around, making space in my head.
The 'I' moves over, a presence is flying my paint — random-like fragments —
hues mating, three-dimensionality accumulating.
Ah, magic."
The Lower East Side, 1986

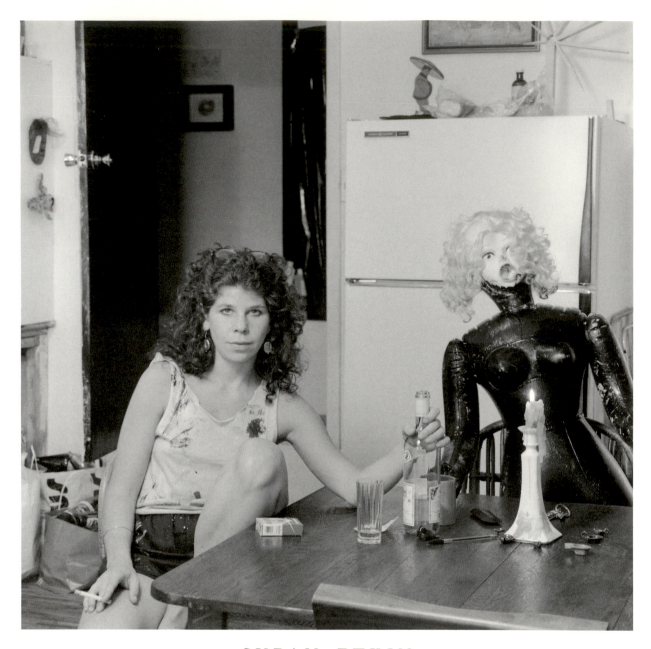

SUZAN ETKIN

After rolling nude in raw paint pigments, she lies on her paintings.
Because laying in toxic paint is unhealthy, someone bought her this blow-up doll.
SoHo, 1984

"FAB•5•FREDDY"

Fred Brathwaite
The world's first rapper, actor, break-dancer, video-jock, graffiti artist.
Williamsburg, Brooklyn, 1985

ERIC FISCHL

He has revived figure painting with strange but recognizable scenarios.
I took Eric to the beach and this scene just "happened."
Far Rockaway, 1982

JANET FISH

Still life.
SoHo, 1986

LOUISE FISHMAN

A second generation painter.
Mother's work is on the wall.
The Meat Market District, West 14 Street, 1983

KENJI FUJITA

Sophisticated artist in assembled wood.
Greenpoint, Brooklyn, 1987

JEDD GARET

Jedd is his own movement.
He considers it great revenge on his teachers that
he has become a serious artist.
The Lower East Side, 1983

SANDY GELLIS

Every day is Earth Day for her.
The Bowery, 1985

HERBERT GENTRY

A beautiful man with beautiful children.
He lived in Paris for many years — an artist in exile.
This is not uncommon for black artists.
West 23 Street, 1986

STEVE GIANAKOS

If there were stand-up artists, he would be King.
Greenwich Village, 1986

DOROTHY GILLESPIE

She gives the impression of purity.
Hell's Kitchen, 1986

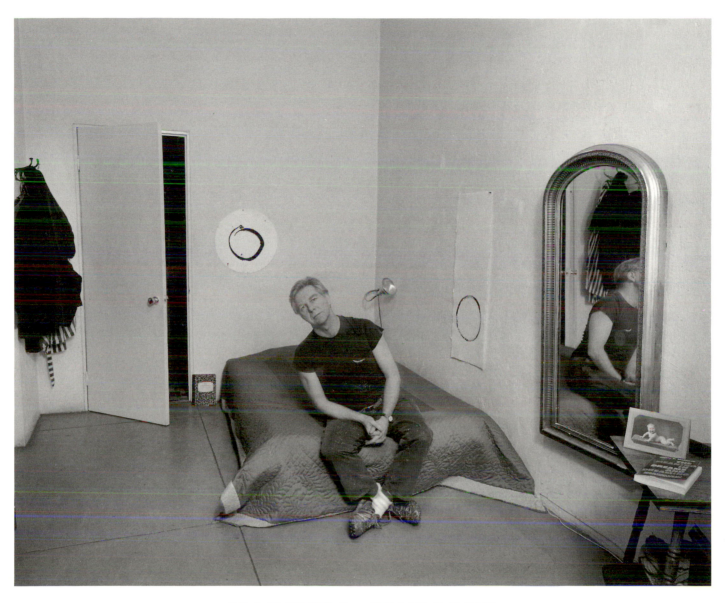

MAXWELL GIMBLETT

An actor in his own play, the bedroom was like a stage set, all the pieces were there.
The Bowery, 1983

JUDY GLANTZMAN

A very typical subject for artists are other artists.
This is how we realize our strength.
The East Village, 1985

MICHAEL GOLDBERG

A feisty, second-generation abstract expressionist
— he can be charming or mad.
Mark Rothko's Old Studio, The Bowery, 1982

JACK GOLDSTEIN

He came from Cal Arts, lives in an old factory,
and works with spray paints and air brushes.
Flatbush, Brooklyn, 1984

LEON GOLUB & NANCY SPERO

They have a twin conscience for a generation hungering for meaningful content.
Brutality, murder, and terrorism are subjects they face together.
Greenwich Village, 1984

GUY GOODWIN

It is hard to imagine someone who more lives his art.
He smells like a fresh oil painting.
The Old West Side Highway, 1983

DENISE GREEN

The circle and square are her riches,
enlivened by a code-like language and color.
Canal Street, 1983

MARCIA GROSTEIN

A well known Brazilian transplant.
Those who know the secrets do not speak.
Upper East Side, 1988

ROBERT GWATHMEY

"There is no such thing as too many artists."
Long Island, 1986

KEITH HARING

Landing somewhere between graffiti and generic,
his art speaks a universal language.
He was outstanding.
The Lower East Side, 1982

JAMES HARRISON

An artist of illuminations,
he was a beatnik, a reformed junkie,
and a hermit with an inimitable personality,
who, by 1990, had worn out his liver.
Greenpoint, Brooklyn, 1982

JOSEPH HASKE

This man holds nothing back.
He lives a struggle too personal for an art crowd looking for a thrill.
Tribeca, 1986

ROBERT HAWKINS

He lives in an abandoned movie theater.
Macho superstars buy his art.
Bleecker Street, 1984

PETER HEINEMANN

I find that artists are the most congenial subjects for a photographer.
They are always obsessed with themselves, which is a catalyst for creativity.
On the surface, all of Peter's paintings are of himself.
Little Italy, 1986

AL HELD

A master of geometric composition,
defining outer space in abstract painting.
West Broadway, 1985

DALE HENRY

"At its best my art is fully considered and remains surfaced.
With the photograph I ask that all ingredients in use be duly
registered without special regard to any one of them."
Upstate New York, 1983

JENE HIGHSTEIN

A sculptor who loves materials and makes choosing them an act of renewal.
Chambers Street, 1982

RUTH BECKHAM HOLLOMAN

Ruth raised her children to become artists —
then she followed in their footsteps.
The Village, 1987

Best wishes on the Best
always,
Ruth Beckham Holloman
Dec. 9, 1991

JENNY HOLZER

Printed signs, electronic billboards, granite benches, and sarcophagi.
The Lower East Side, 1985

REBECCA HOWLAND

Her work deals with corruption,
greed, and environmental disasters
yet contains a reflection of maternal beauty.
That which builds up at the same time tears down;
that which breaks at the same time reconstructs.
We always fought, but stayed close friends.
Franklin Street, 1983

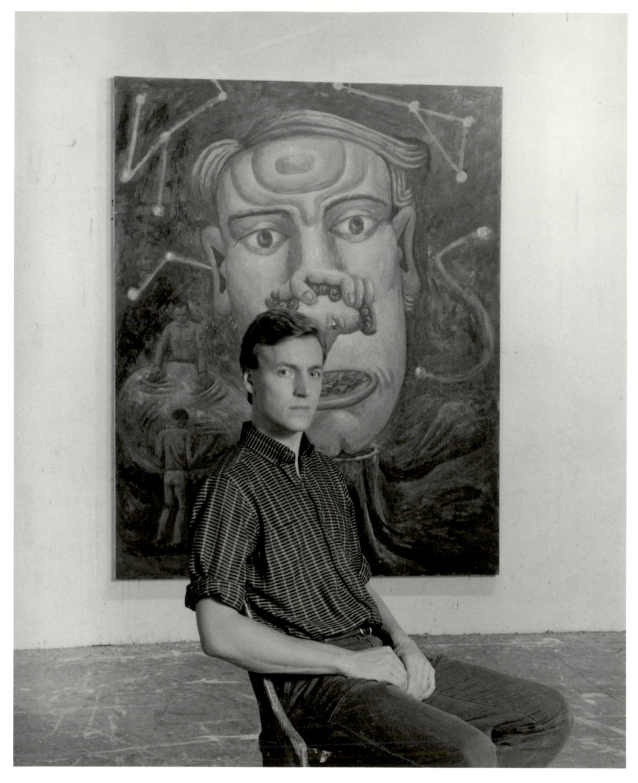

DAVID HUMPHREY

An associate of the distinguished David McGee Gallery.
Artists often work in museums and art galleries;
creative tensions — creative controls.
The Meat Market District, West 14 Street, 1986

WILL INSLEY

Clean, geometric, what he describes is not of this planet.
Initially a minimalist, he became involved in creating a city, and therefore a society.
The perfect world — like Saint Joan of Arc — tied to a stake.
The Bowery, 1983

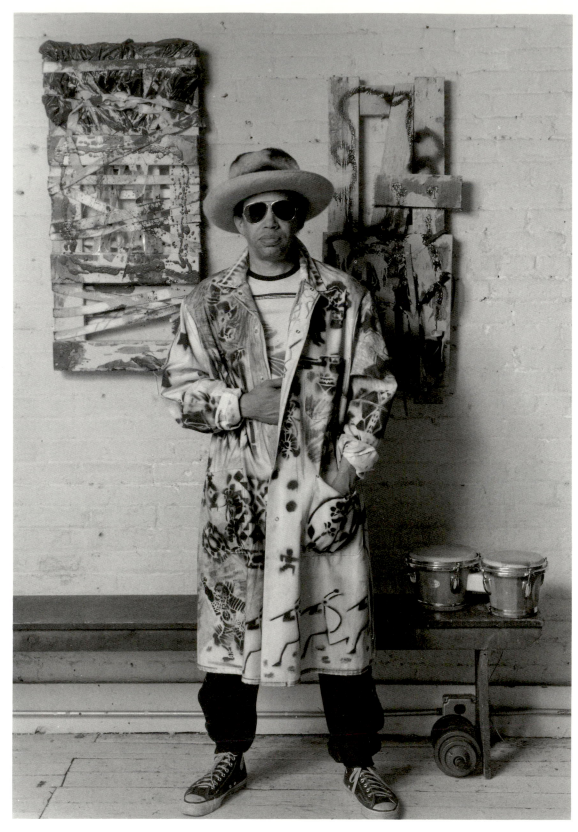

GERALD JACKSON

A man, happy on the border, wearing his own creation.
He spends time in Europe with an international artists set.
The Bowery, 1987

NOAH JEMISON

His paintings first appear to be abstract.
Then images begin emerging — romantic scenarios of daily life.
He directed the Bronx River Museum.
Williamsburg, Brooklyn, 1986

BILL JENSEN

A main artist source for The Artist Project. *He is a recluse and*
only agreed to this portrait knowing I would then photograph
the artists that he felt were important to the book.
A circuitous route, but well worth it.
Williamsburg, Brooklyn, 1983

JOAN JONAS

A performance artist and member of the "Mercer Street Women's Group."
SoHo, 1985

KIM JONES

He is a performance artist — primal, tribal, aboriginal, therapeutic.
Having seen the worst the world has to offer, in Vietnam,
he is giving it back his best.
Myrtle Avenue, Brooklyn, 1987

ROBERTO JUAREZ

Successful and well connected but not the kind to make a lot of noise about it.
Clearly, he also understands the conscious and unconscious aims
of those who came before him.
His paintings are achievements of a man who knows his own mind.
East Houston Street, 1982

DAVID KAPP

A Long Islander whose parents collect art,
married to an artist who is the daughter of an artist,
he paints the grid of the city.
Greenpoint, Brooklyn, 1982

ALEX KATZ

"American cheese on white bread is the ultimate."
One of the most understated artists in this country today.
West Broadway, 1985

HERBERT KATZMAN

Balzac in Manhattan.
Westbeth, Greenwich Village, 1986

MINORU KAWABATA

He is from Japan and guards himself somewhat.
A very sincere artist and teacher at the New School with a loyal following of students.
Westbeth, Greenwich Village, 1986

STEVE KEISTER

Sculpture can be made of anything,
sit upon the floor, spook you like a UFO.
A most unique and sensitive man, quiet within the horror.
Tribeca, 1982

CHRISTOF KOHLHOFER

German, very comic, able to laugh at death.
SoHo, 1984

KOMAR & MELAMID

A couple of regular collaborative artists from the Eastern Bloc.
East 36 Street, 1985

JEFF KOONS

*Andy Warhol's "nephew" is
the Michael Jackson of appropriation,
making banal objects of the world into limited edition icons.
SoHo, 1984*

HARRIET KORMAN

She and her work seem to vibrate like a cosmic "Om."
Williamsburg, 1983

JOSEPH KOSUTH

His work deals with language and is so intelligent I wonder who understands it.
A macho genius by reputation, who dresses only in black
and is not to be messed with.
SoHo, 1983

GARY B. KUEHN

Besides making sculpture, his passion is building boats.
Chelsea, 1985

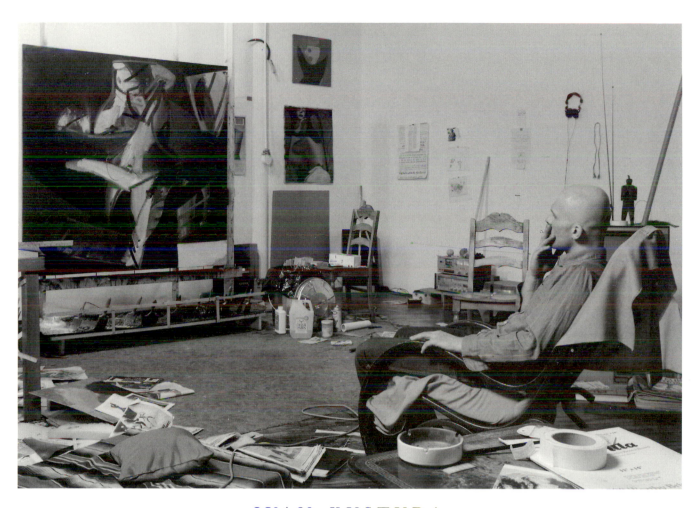

IVAN KUSTURA

*He retains a flair as an eccentric European,
but like many artists from the Eastern Bloc,
he is conventional in his views.
Greenpoint, Brooklyn, 1986*

"LADY PINK"

Sandra Fabara & HB

A beautiful young woman who became a celebrated graffiti artist,
and helped the street life of the boroughs gain
the attention of the world.
Jackson Heights, Queens, 1985

DAVID LAWLESS

He is his own piece, his dog is epileptic.
Tribeca, 1982

THOMAS LAWSON

His art — politically challenging — questions our beliefs.
Though low-key in person, when he speaks his Scottish accent makes wonderful sounds.
The Financial District, 1982

CATHERINE LEE

A determined Texas woman came to New York, established herself as an abstract artist,
and maintains fiercely her own identity in the territory.
Tribeca, 1982

DON LEICHT

His work is cut from metal.
Its theme is its relation to you,
where you are, and where your family is in society.
The Bronx, 1982

ANNETTE LEMIEUX

A conceptualist with a great sense of beauty and history.
Chinatown, 1985

JACK LEVINE

*A tough, angry guy
who is not a social realist.
Greenwich Village, 1986*

LES LEVINE

*He projects a sense of control
over how he sees and how he thinks.
Chelsea, 1985*

MARGRIT LEWCZUK

Art itself created Margrit, who is passionately
responding to its challenge to return the soul to the world.
The Meat Market District, West 14 Street, 1985

DONALD LIPSKI

He lives in a madcap world of assemblage,
sort of Rube Goldberg does Duchamp, with an intensity of the wry.
Greenpoint, Brooklyn, 1987

ROBERT LONGO

A kid from Brooklyn with a strong belief in
the idea that he can have it all.
South Street Seaport, 1984

WHITFIELD LOVELL

Everything comes up pleasure in Lovell's world.
His art is an examination of his past.
The East Village, 1987

MICHAEL LUCERO

A sculptor who combines Southwestern imagery with information from another planet.
He zooms out of the crafts category.
Chelsea, 1987

ROBERT MANGOLD

Lots of ovals
ovals everywhere
— themselves a source of energy —
central points by which
everything else
is measured.
Upstate New York, 1984

BRICE MARDEN

He became respected as an artist in the 60s.
When I shot this Marden was doing sketches for a cathedral . . .
in the ancestral relationship of artist and church.
The Bowery, 1985

CHRIS MARTIN

Innocent art with mastery and power.
Greenpoint, Brooklyn, 1984

HOWARD MCCALEBB

" Idiosyncratic purities, intellectual query, study everything.
If I come across something that excites me, I try to make art, learn things first thing."
Tribeca, 1986

ALLAN MCCOLLUM

One of my heros, very dedicated. His subject — the subjectless.
His endless series stands for the void, for the universal expression of all art.
It has made him famous.
SoHo, 1982

GEORGE MCNEIL

He has toughed it out and survived as an abstract artist.
A teacher at Pratt, he has his studio in an old carriage house nearby.
His face makes me think of Plato.
Clinton Hill, Brooklyn, 1985

TAYLOR MEAD

He is quite a well-known personality in New York City
and the author of a brilliant book, Taylor Mead on Amphetamine and in Europe.
In love with everyone and everything, he was a good friend of Andy Warhol's.
The Lower East Side, 1984

SAM MESSER

An experienced expressionist in vivid color.
He probed the psyche, played the casinos in Atlantic City,
and moved to California.
P.S.1, Long Island City, Queens, 1984

ANN MESSNER

She does metal sculpture in which I can feel her small boy's toys and her art interplay.
The Lower East Side, 1984

MELISSA MEYER

She is an abstract painter with noble Renaissance sources. The paintings are powerful.
Tribeca, 1985

MARILYN MINTER

She came to New York from Louisiana in 1976 and became involved
with the group who did the "Terminal Shows" in abandoned New York buildings.
She describes her work as "exquisite corpses."
Mercer Street, 1984

IRIS MITCHELL

A story worthy of Baudelaire or Zola.
"Discovered" selling small paintings on the streets of the city, she was a heroin addict who
had had a heartbreaking childhood but still was very creative, very artistic.
She became "known." They began to show her art in New York galleries, and she was
awarded a scholarship to study at Pratt Institute.
But the drug wouldn't let go of her.
Inevitably, she was homeless and diseased and died with AIDS.
I had to identify her body at the City Morgue — wishing she could have stayed longer.
The Lower East Side, 1985

NANCY MITCHNICK

It is strange the things that influence an artist:
a list of book titles, Degas flowers on the mantel.
The West Side, 1985

RICHARD MOCK

To him creativity seems to feed on excess and conflict, conflicting with whatever yokes its power.
A link between Genie und Irrsin, "the lunatic/the lover/the poet," he gives us the feeling that
the creative thrives best at the destructive frontier, close to evil, close to death.
The Brooklyn Waterfront, 1985

PAUL MOGENSEN

An artist's artist doing pure work at a profound level,
undistracted by life's interruptions or corruptions.
SoHo, 1985

FRANK MOORE

A real native, born in New York City.
He studied at Yale University and
Cite des Arts in Paris.
SoHo, 1986

MALCOLM MORLEY

Little gremlins are dancing around his head.
SoHo, 1985

KATHY MUEHLEMANN

A careful painter of the cosmos.
It is remarkable where such small paintings can send you.
Canal Street, 1984

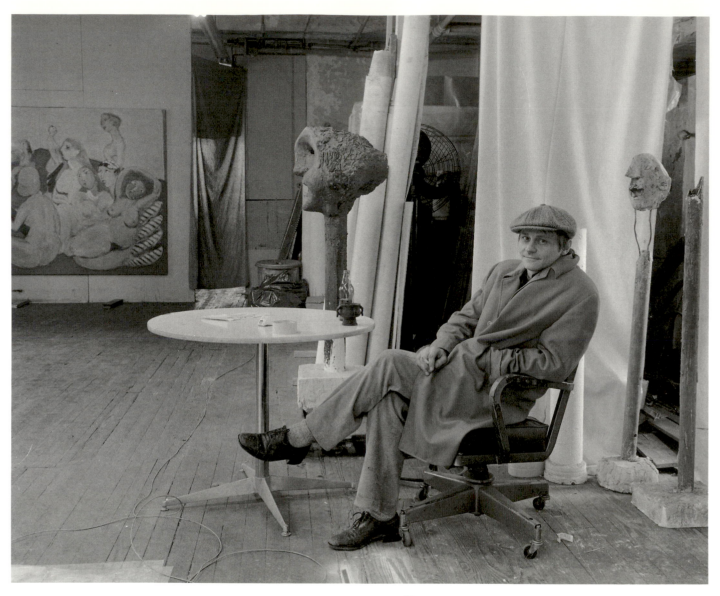

GREGOIRE MÜLLER

European artists tend to be more introspective than American artists,
less polluted by the media; yet American culture is pervasive.
SoHo, 1982

ELIZABETH MURRAY

She is seen as the leader of women artists, but despite her prestige,
she is down-to-earth and very matter-of-fact.
Tribeca, 1985

REUBEN NAKIAN

One of the most distinguished sculptors of the 20th century,
the son of an immigrant, he grew up in New York City
and found his mature style after 50 — a style at once heroic and painterly.
At the age of 89 he allowed me this moment,
not long before he died.
Connecticut, 1986

JOSEPH NECHVATAL

A graduate of Columbia University he does simple yet deep drawings, sketches of psychological states.
57 Street Gallery, 1983

JOHN NEWMAN

Yale seems to have a way of making successful artists.
John describes his art as "The imagery of organic forms of nature, cellular principles of matter."
Tribeca, 1987

RICHARD NONAS

A macho man with whimsy.
He can make a rock express itself.
Tribeca, 1982

THOMAS NOZKOWSKI

Abstraction like it used to be; a way to express impossible relationships.
He has extensive contacts with many other abstract artists.
They show their kinship by trading their work with each
other and some of these works appear in this photo.
His studio is in an old synagogue.
The Lower East Side, 1983

JOHN OBUCK

"The paintings are about detachment and involvement.
I show objects existing and relating to other objects.
I am interested in space, balance, and harmony
and the resulting eccentricity of those ingredients."
Tribeca, 1982

PAT OLESZKO

The best of the great performance artists.
A genius with costumes and startling props, she reaches all the way out.
Tribeca, 1987

LUIGI ONTANI

An Italian who frequented the city
— a unique individual living a psychosexually ambivalent existence.
Tribeca, 1985

LORENZO PACE

He does large installation pieces which deal with drugs, voodoo,
African tribal influences, art as medicinal, shamanistic, alchemical —
all the cultural influences to which he has been exposed.
Williamsburg, 1986

RAY PARKER

An abstract expressionist from the 50s.
He exposes his soul in his paintings and it stays with you.
SoHo, 1985

PAT PASSLOF

An intense, respected, veteran painter, and friend to many unknown artists.
She prefers the underground.
The Lower East Side, 1985

PHILIP PAVIA

"Artists are warriors."
He was another member of the notorious
"Tenth Street Gang."
Broadway, 1986

BEVERLY PEPPER

A tough lady doing huge, tough art.
Tribeca, 1986

VICTOR PESCE

A former plumber and regular guy, Victor discovered the re-creation of the individual,
— the mystery of art —
Connecticut, 1985

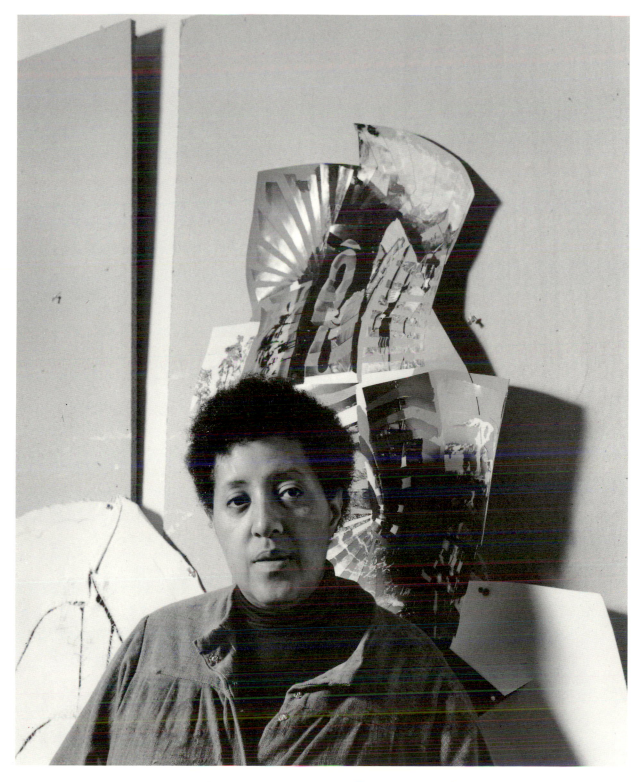

HOWARDENA PINDELL

All is material for her elaborate slices of life and nothing escapes her.
SoHo, 1986

ALYSON POU

*She is a performance artist as well as
an administrator for a performing arts company.
The shrine is in her small, one room, tenement apartment;
a ritualistic setting with a mirror for reflection.
Lower East Side, 1987*

LUCIO POZZI

In a studio bustling with assistants, he has taken huge artistic steps,
while being concerned with the often overlooked.
I caught him in a rare quiet moment,
sorting watercolors.
SoHo, 1983

REBECCA PURDUM

One of the wonders of the art world, she paints with her fingers.
Beautiful, soulful, abstract works — subtle fogs of color.
Chelsea, 1986

HARVEY QUAYTMAN

His paintings have "holes" in them and are filled with
the recapitulated history of abstraction.
The Bowery, 1984

RAQUEL RABINOVICH

"In my glass sculpture I explore and search for metaphorical space
capable of embracing paradox, of being at once inside and outside.
My work attempts to reveal the presence of the absence,
the 'Sanctum Sanctorum,' of what is seen but not known."
SoHo, 1987

DAVID RABINOWITCH

*A careful, calculating, but visionary sculptor whose every word
is as carefully measured as his work.
East Houston, 1984*

DAVID REED

The luscious feeling of Neapolitan painting was his vision,
with modern precision.
Tribeca, 1983

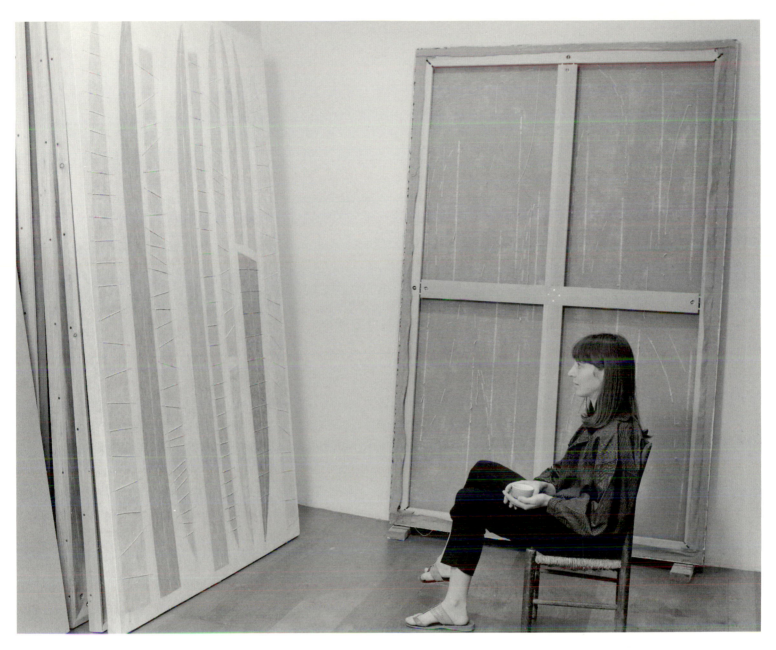

EDDA RENOUF

The daughter of an artist, her apartment and her paintings
are filled with archeological antiquities.
She is quiet and unpretentious.
Fifth Avenue, 1985

PAUL RESIKA

An artist of the old school and a constant impressionist
(not the French kind), he impressed himself *upon the canvas.*
He had an admiring student there.
His studio bed indicated that
he truly lived his art.
Upper West Side, 1986

MILTON RESNICK

An astute eminence, he produces incredibly tactile paintings.
I had the camera set up and made this first casual shot when the phone rang
with some horrendous news. That ended the shoot.
The Lower East Side, 1984

CONNIE REYES

She had a studio below her significant other, Ronnie Bladen.
Together they were a force. The sculpture here was built into her loft
— like a rendition of her drawings. The whole thing was spring loaded and shaking.
Fifth Avenue, 1983

JUDY RIFKA

She rode into the decade on a wave of new imagery
through the "Times Square Show,"
a platform for many artists.
Tribeca, 1982

FAITH RINGGOLD

A widely acclaimed artist and the winner of a Guggenheim.
Harlem, 1985

WALTER ROBINSON

A critic and artist,
his paintings comment on the social scene of the day.
He said, "photographs are too easy to be an art form,"
which made me very amused.
Tribeca, 1983

HERMAN ROSE

He has a magnificent ability to portray the beauty of the world on canvas.
We got along well — a mutual admiration for the work we're both doing.
Westbeth, Greenwich Village, 1985

SUSAN ROTHENBERG

One of the most acclaimed artists of the 80s.
She is a dedicated painter, not an art star playing the publicity machine.
Her work is gained from a sea of subconscious images
emerging onto a conscious surface.
Tribeca, 1985

ED RUDA

A minimalist,
married to a Mescalero Apache Indian actress.
Tribeca, 1987

CHRISTY RUPP

Her work deals with the poisoning of our environment.
Much of the imagery involves animals in an urban jungle:
monkeys under bridges, dragons in alleys,
giant trouts in sewers.
The Financial District, 1983

PAUL RUSSOTTO

He views as his mentors the artists from the "Tenth Street Gang,"
who he invites over to criticize his work.
East 10 Street, 1987

ALISON SAAR

I photographed her shortly after she arrived in New York City.
She explores folk art with a contemporary freshness.
Her objects seem charmed, blessed with aliveness.
Chelsea, 1985

KENNY SCHARF

Comic, erotic art using the common expressions of the day.
The child and the shadow.
The Clock Tower, 1983

SEAN SCULLY

Stripes, nothing but stripes, and so diverse, so intriguing
— a painter of ambition.
Tribeca, 1982

CHARLES SEARLES

*He left me with an appreciation for the tradition
of identity, culture, heritage, Africa.
Greenwich Village, 1987*

RICHARD SERRA

Cold-rolled steel.
The 800 pound gorilla expanded,
put the kick in any environment.
The most controversial sculptor of the decade.
Tribeca, 1985

JOEL SHAPIRO

With the ability to create an object that deserves endless contemplation,
his work is respected and collected.
A comfortable man.
Bleecker Street, 1985

JUDITH SHEA

She understands the expressiveness of clothes and torsos and metaphor.
The way to be sensitized to her sculpture is by touching
and running your hand along the volume of a piece.
Tribeca, 1984

CINDY SHERMAN

The endless theater of her self-portraiture
has unleashed an extraordinary creativity
of which the art world can't get enough.
South Street Seaport, 1983

LEE SHERRY

She wants to express herself, unpretentious and exposed to the world.
A bath is a pleasant place to do this.
Chinatown, 1985

LAURIE SIMMONS

Using photography to reflect a middle-class existence
— accomplished through a surreal world of dolls,
she has expanded into mannequins and dancing cameras.
SoHo, 1982

She was no more
exotic than the
sparse room
she posed in

LORNA SIMPSON

Under the rubric of conceptual art,
photography is no longer a bastard medium,
but an expressive image-making process.
I think of her as a work of her own art.
P.S.1, Long Island City, Queens, 1988

CLARISSA T. SLIGH

She makes childlike art.
Doesn't creativity also have a childhood?
SoHo, 1988

KIKI SMITH

A fountain of creative talent and Bohemian life-style,
she is definitive of the Lower East Side.
Making sculpture out of biological fact,
Kiki did a pregnancy piece which
brought itself to full term.
The Lower East Side, 1983

LEON POLK SMITH

He is like a wise, old Indian.
From the Great Plains.
Union Square, 1986

VINCENT D. SMITH

*Each room of his studio contains a different aspect of his career.
He is soulful and introspective; seems at peace with himself,
able to channel all of his thoughts into his work.
Downtown, Brooklyn, 1987*

JOSEPH SOLMAN

A fine colorist, Solman draws supremely well,
and proves it in the sure outlines of his portraits,
many of which he has done as a result of frequent trips to
The Aqueduct Racetrack.
The Bowery, 1986

EVE SONNEMAN

A photographer is primarily a focused eye.
Sonneman is all-seeing, even the most common subjects attain elegance.
Tribeca, 1987

KEITH SONNIER

One hard-bitten, original, minimalist sculptor — edged in neon.
From New Orleans, his Cajun ways seduced my camera.
Tribeca, 1983

HELEN SOREFF

In the work you see Mondrian at first, then a unique power,
a Michelangelo Starman drawing.
Little Italy, 1984

RAPHAEL SOYER

He traded his country of Russia for his country of New York.
In the late 40s, he was the city's most important artist.
Upper West Side, 1985

HAIM STEINBACH

Out on the edge,
with the detritus of our day
(plus exotic twists)
ranked there one-two-three.
Greenpoint, Brooklyn, 1985

EDVINS STRAUTMANIS

Painting with everything imaginable, even a broom,
he works inside a plastic chamber.
But paint is everywhere!
SoHo, 1986

MICHELLE STUART

She dove into nature leaving no stone unturned.
Her style is visceral with a variety of surfaces
often in mixed media, including shell, soil, and flower petals.
SoHo, 1984

GEORGE SUGARMAN

He exercised a powerful force on the art world for many years,
for which he is fiercely proud.
South Broadway, 1985

KUNIÉ SUGIURA

. . . from Japan in 1967 to The Village.
She has worked in many unusual mediums.
At one time she created images in a darkroom,
painting on photo-sensitive surfaces with chemicals.
In another group of work she did rubber paintings which were
images of fear connected to atomic bombs dropping on her homeland.
Chinatown, 1982

DONALD SULTAN

*Reasoned, yet funny, he understands that the landscape
most of us live with is made of linoleum and tar.
Tribeca, 1983*

TARO SUZUKI

He makes sculpture that examines light reflected by mirrors within a confined space,
creating a supernatural presence.
The East Village, 1982

JORGE TACLA

Many South Americans came to New York City in the mid 80s.
In the arts, divisions of nationality are not barriers, but bridges for expansion.
Tribeca, 1987

BILL TAGGART

An abstract expressionist who paints beyond the walls.
SoHo, 1982

MICHAEL TETHEROW

His works are portraits of what is below the skin, what is beyond matter.
He lives in a wild and windy loft, where he has built tent-like
substructures to keep himself warm.
Tribeca, 1985

PAUL THEK

*"He was one of the most interesting American artists of his generation. . . His extravagant objects reflected
the idealism and the manic, troubling energy of the 60s counterculture."* Holland Cotter, *Art Critic*

This famous underground artist traveled the world.
His elaborate, metaphorical objects were rare treasures,
but most of his large-scale work has, unfortunately, not survived because of neglect.
He died with AIDS. Much of what survives, found in a 5' x 10' locker, was stored by Thek himself.
A Roof Garden, Lower East Side, 1986

HANNE TIERNEY

She makes intriguing puppet theater and performs widely on the art circuit.
The puppets are assembled from objects found in the streets.
The endless hours children spend delving into their
imaginations never seem to end for artists.
East Village, 1982

ESTEBAN VICENTE

A stately gentleman in his 80s who paints every day.
He is an advocate of the sublime side of abstract expressionism — the glow.
Times Square, 1985

JULIE WACHTEL

A graduate of the Whitney Museum program.
When I saw the emblem of the wings on the table,
I couldn't help but use it to express her angelic quality.
Greenpoint, Brooklyn, 1985

ANDY WARHOL

Andy evolved
as the decades evolved.
When he died he was seen as
an American kid from Pennsylvania
who came from a typical family, and
a vessel for American culture in every decade he traversed;
he understood the media and turned the mirror to art.
This picture is Andy on his way to heaven:
creativity in an upward sweep.
Central Park West, 1987

SUSAN WEIL

In her book Birdsong's Heartbeats *she says —*
"The joyous freedom of flight is an expression of my life as an artist.
The experience of making paintings that stand for one's self and one's life
is a mirror that reflects the image of the mind.
I am a phoenix as I was reborn in fire."
Brooklyn, 1984

LAWRENCE WEINER

*An arsenal of press-on letters
results in aphorisms and conundrum —
he is both alchemist and trickster.
Bleecker Street, 1984*

JAMES WELLING

He takes subjectless photos, a masterful achievement.
From grains of dust on velvet, to black jello, to crumbled aluminum,
he has accomplished a remarkable feat in turning these into aesthetic statements.
SoHo, 1982

JACK WHITTEN

Few men I have met had as much character, charm, and courage.
Painter, sculptor, and survivor, this man lost two studios to fire, only to rekindle his career.
The tools and instruments he uses, such as a series of wooden combs, come from his African heritage.
They create a hypnotic, layered effect of stripes with depth.
Tribeca, 1983

THORNTON WILLIS

*"Abstract painting has always interested me because it offers the broadest means to express
universal qualities and values . . . remains international in style, and holds to certain
expressionist tenets which for me are more clearly and purely held to through a non-representational means."*
SoHo, 1984

JACKIE WINDSOR

Originally a process
sculptor she proves
one can do a simple
cube two thousand
& 1 complex ways.
SoHo,   1984

ROBIN WINTERS

*Part fairy tale, part symbolist, Winter's art seduces the audience
takes them away, and then dumps them into their current circumstance.
SoHo, 1983*

TERRY WINTERS

A successful painter who came from Brooklyn and went to Pratt Institute.
He has created a personalized vocabulary; a language in paint.
Tribeca, 1987

MARTIN WONG

He is much like his sign-language paintings.
At his first show, he gave all of his work away
to strangers in the street.
Chinatown, 1985

BOB YASUDA

Delicious abstraction.
He is from Hawaii and imported some of its luxuriant spirit.
SoHo, 1983

ROBERT YUCIKAS

New York monuments seen through filled mazes,
often with a diamond in the sky.
The Bowery, 1983

JOE ZUCKER

He creates new imagery and uses new materials.
The painting behind him is made of wax and pigment.
East Hampton, 1987

MICHAEL ZWACK

He makes dream-like forms and appears to be in a dream state himself.
The Lower East Side, 1985

EPILOGUE

New York Artists : The Eighties

Many artists believe New York to be the center of their big dream. Endless lines of people from Texas to Tacoma, from Mississippi to Massachusetts stream into this city. For each there is a perpetual beating and straining as he or she attempts to find a place among so many other creative souls.

From the beginning I was attracted to artists and their energy; that rigidly individual, sometimes impatient, yet always soulful and intensely human quality they share. Theirs is a life of investigation and discovery, and so, too, I was drawn to find out more about them. I soon reached the point where I discovered that is how they felt about the work themselves: that they live through their creations. I wanted to capture and exhibit a record of this in a way that would show that these are ordinary people from every walk of life who share an extraordinary love for the ephemeral.

My life as a photographer began in the seventh grade. I took pictures of hippies in Central Park playing bongos, and there I met a commercial photographer, Roger Pregint, an immigrant from France. He came to see my pictures. He showed me his pictures. I was hired as his assistant, sweeping the studio floor, loading his camera, making contact prints. I kept making pictures of my own. I recorded the streets of Manhattan and Brooklyn, where I went to college at Pratt Institute. I started doing portraits of my friends and family, and Roger's many friends. I freelanced as a photographer's assistant to learn, and sought out my own photo jobs in dance, theater, the arts.

In 1982 I got a call from a friend of Orson Welles. She had some sculpture in Orson's apartment—would I come photograph them? I was excited by the prospect of meeting the Genius, himself. The glamour soon evaporated when I saw him, a man who could barely walk, with too many frailties, lots of pain and medication. The pictures of the sculpture were hard work, but I was able to ask for Orson's portrait. I went to the Carlyle at 11:30 one morning. He appeared in a large bath robe and told me which side of his profile to photograph. I took both sides in fifteen or twenty minutes. He was obsessed with lighting.

When I sent the pictures to him in California, he sent me back a job offer as a cameraman on his next movie. I would have been excited, but instead I remembered his difficulties in moving about. I kept to myself and then took a cross-country trip, ending up in Los Angeles, but I didn't look him up. When I returned to New York, he called me to ask for a portrait of his wife. I gave him two estimates. He said they were too high, and he'd call me again when I learned to give a proper estimate. I thought again about going to him, about movie-making. Somehow he was too frail, I felt unable to give up my ties to family and friends in the East to go to him. Not long after, he died.

ORSON WELLES, 1982

The experience with Orson left me longing for something. Perhaps it was the way he took command of the situation, his intense theatricality. He was an outlaw, and did not play the game of life the same way others did. He became the Archetype. Though I knew nothing about the New York art scene, I wanted to photograph the people who existed in that world who, like Orson, had frailties, but were obsessed by the creative spirit. I set out to take portraits of every artist in New York. I believed that if people could look at my pictures they could know what art was through the individuals that make it.

The Artist Project was a coming of age for me. I learned there was more to photography than just taking shots, for as much as the operation of the camera was a skill I possess, the real talent necessary was in human relations. I had envisioned the project a taking, not creating. The artists were to be my victims. But I was overtaken by the subjects of my choosing, and it was as if I had handed myself over to them and they directed me, or rejected me. Now I wonder who was used by whom. — Peter

PETER BELLAMY 1991 — *Prigent*

A Note of Thanks

The following are some of the people who helped make The Artist Project happen. Without them, and many others, none of this would have been possible.

Many thanks! I especially want to thank William Zimmer who believed in the project from the beginning and saw me through it all.

Audrey and Chris Abbott
Mary Abbott
Kim Abraham
Alice Adams
Charlie Ahearn
John Ahearn
Paul King Akin
John Alexander
Vikhy Alexander
Julia Allard
Gregory Amenoff
William Anastasi
Stephen Antonakos
Geraldine Aramanda
Arman
Richard Armijo
Carl Ashby
Dan Asher
Michel Auder
Barry X Ball
Will Barnet
Frances Barth
Jack Barth
Bill Beckley
Alan Belcher
Gayer Bellamy, Jr.
Hannah Bellamy
Richard Bellamy
Robyn Bellamy
Wilder Bellamy
Lynda Benglis
Ellen Berkenblit
Rosann Berry
Jake Berthot
Natvar Bhavsar
Tom Bills
Virginia K. Bolton
Bomb Magazine
David Bowes
James Bowness
Paul Brach
Laura Bradley
Dove Bradshaw
Glenn Branca
Troy Brauntuch
James Brown
Jerry Buchanan

Howard Buchwald
Edgar Buonagurio
Toby Buonagurio
Gary Burnly
Michael J. Byron
Sarah Canright
Christopher Cantwell
Marina Cappelletto
Ernst Caramelle
Laurel Carroll
Joseph Chassler
Rhys Chatham
John Cheim
The Clock Tower
Chuck Close
Charles Clough
Peter Coates
Co-Lab
Arch Connelly
Pierluigi Consagra
Jay Coogan
Denise Corley
Michael Corris
Jane Couch
Crash
Thom Cooney Crawford
Susan Crile
William Crozier
Emilio Cruz
Jody Culkin
Thomas F. Cunningham
Marcia Dalby
Karen Chamber Dalton
Debby Davis
Michael Davis
Daze
Robert De Niro
Bridget De Socio
Larry Deyab
Martha Diamond
Jane Dickson
Baldo Diodato
John E. Dobbs
Garrick Dolberg
Hector Dowd
Peter Downsborough
Tom Doyle

Jorg Dubin
Joe Dugan
Duke University Union Galleries
Fontaine Dunn
Elizabeth Dworkin
Mary Beth Edelson
Natalie Edgar
Elliott Erwitt
Fred Esher
Geneen Estrada
Corinne Etienne
Gretchen Faust
Sandi Fellman
Herbert Ferber
Rafael Ferrer
Louis Finkelstein
Craig Fisher
Kent Floeter
James L. Ford
John Ford
Stephen Frailey
Sondra Freckelton
Suzan Frecon
Joe Fyfe
Bobbie G.
Brian Gayman
Sonia Gechtoff
Dana Geltner
Dina Ghen
Kathleen Gilje
Madelynn Gingold
Mike Glier
Sharon Gold
Kathy Goodell
Marian Goodman Gallery
Lee Gordon
April Gornik
Gerry Gorovoy
Elka Gould
Mr. and Mrs. Mark Gould
Dan Graham
Rodney Greenblat
Bobby Grenier
Robert Grosvenor
Sue Ferguson Gussow
Ira Joel Haber
David Hacker

Marcia Hafif
Joellen Hall
Peter Halley
Mary Hambleton
Freya Hansell
Dean Hartung
Michael Harvey
David Hatchett
Don Hazlitt
Michael Heizer
Margaret Lee Henderson
Lynda Herrera
James Hill
Robin Hill
James Hillman
Stewart Hitch
Barry Holden
Robin Holder
Nanch Holt
Elizabeth Howard
Jean Hoyt
Holly Hughes
Ralph Humphrey
Jim Huntington
Michael Hurson
Ellen Hutchinson
Paolo Icaro
Mark Innerst
Alfredo Jaar
Ron Janowich
Valerie Jaudon
Suzanne Joelson
Monique Johannet
Alan Johnston
Claudio Juárez
Brandt Juncean
Cecily Kahn
Stan Ford Kay
Mel Kendrick
Kent Fine Art
Vivian Kerstein
Malcolm Kesselman
Michael Kessler
Frederick Koch
Bill Komoski
Joyce Kozloff
Eddie Kunze

Ted Kurahara
Robert Kushner
Stephen Lack
Wolfgang Laib
Lois Lane
Larry Lang
The Lanman Companies
Brooke Larsen
Rex Lau
LedisFlam Gallery
Barry Ledoux
Colin Lee
John Lees
Ed Leffingwell
Julian Lethbridge
Jeffrey Lew
Robert Lobe
Fern H. Logan
Lulu Lopez
Mark Lyon
Frances Lyshak
Chris MacDonald
Steven Madoff
Gerald Marcus
Joseph Marioni
Jim Martin
Barry McCallion
Jan McCartin
William McCartin
Ron McQueen
Amanda Means
Goren Medak
The Menil Foundation
Linda Jane Mercer
Richard T. Miller
Robert Miller
Robert Miller Gallery
Keith Milow
Richard Minsky
Iris Mitchell
Fashion Moda
Phyllis Moore
Carmen Gloria Morales
Anthony Morrell
Oliver Mosset
Steven Mueller
Matt Mullican

Judith Murray
The Museum of Modern Art
Forrest Myers
Peter Nadin
Peter Nagy
Jiro Naito
Don Nice
Costantino Nivola
Alex Nixon
NOC
Cady Noland
Kenneth Noland
David Novros
Doug Ohlson
Oil and Steel Gallery
Bobbie Oliver
Alfonso Ossorio
Trina And Mike Overlock
P.S.1
Henry Pearson
George Peck
Ellen Phelan
Massimo Pierucci
Amos Poe
Roger Prigent
Richard Prince
Roger Prinz
Richard Pugliese
Jim Reed
Bill Rice
Dan Rizzi
Bruce Robbins
Michael Robbins
Debby Roberts
Joyce Robins
Walter Robinson
Dorothea Rockburne
Mary Anne Rose
Jane Rosen
James Rosenquist
Stephan Rosenthal
Paul Rotterdam
Bonnie Rychlak
Nieves Saah
Juliet and Serafin Saenz
Jonathan Santlofer
Michel Sauer

David Saunders
Margo Sawyer
Art Schade
Miriam Schapiro
Robert Schiffmacher
Frank Schroeder
Peter Schuff
Charles Schwefel
George Segal
Tony Shafrazi
Dena Shottenkirk
Frances Siegel
Carol Skaff
Sandy Skoglund
Robert Slutzky
Bernard E. Smith, Jr.
Mr. and Mrs. Bernard E. Smith, III
Jean Ford Smith
Michael Smith
Mike Smith
Richard Smith
Stephanie Jo Smith
Susan Smith
Kenneth Snelson
Joan Snitzer
Joan Snyder
D. Jack Solomon
Eve Sonneman
Olga Spiegel
Robert Stackhouse
Jolie Stahl
Ted Stamm
Hedda Sterne
May Stevens
Marianne Stikas
William Stone
Robert Storr
Betsy Sussler
Jim Swank
Christopher Sweet
Mark Tansey
Al C. Taylor
Michael Tetherow
Robin Tewes
Texas Photo Type
Joan Thorne
Edward Thorp Gallery

Sidney Tillim
Connie Rogers Tilton
Jack Tilton
Jack Tilton Gallery
Rick Tilton
Kenneth Tisi
Hap Tivey
Tabo Toral
John E. Torreano
Diane Townsend
Stefan Triffa
Trine and Brenda
David True
Anne Turyn
Allan Uglow
United States General Services Administration
—Emma Gomez
Clover Vail
Hank Virgona
Merrill Wagner
The Andy Warhol Foundation
Tom Warren
Jeffrey Wasserman
Jonathan Waters
Marc Weber
Meg Webster
Bill Wegman
Victoria Weill
James Welling
Orson Welles
David West
Stephen Westfall
Hannah Williams
Wendy Williams
Jane Wilson
Bob Witz
Dan Witz
Tod Wizon
Steve Wood
Tom Woodruff
Mrs. Helen Wright
Daisy Youngblood
Jack Youngerman
Adja Yunkers
Barbara Zucker

INDEX

LIST OF ILLUSTRATIONS

SANDER, August. pg. 7
The Painter Gottfried Brockmann (1924) from the series *Citizens of the 20th Century*, from the portfolio *Painters and Sculptors*.
Gelatin - silver print, 10 x 7 3/8".
Collection, The Museum of Modern Art, New York.
Gift of Gerd Sander.